With Thanks

DAN SAGE

With Thanks
© Dan Sage 2022, All rights reserved
www.dansageauthor.com
facebook.com/dansageauthor
@dansageauthor

First edition: December 2022
Cover: James, Go On Write
ISBN: 978-0-6452742-4-0 (epub)
ISBN: 978-0-6452742-6-4 (paperback)

Cataloguing-in-Publication details are available from the National Library of Australia
www.trove.nla.gov.au

By this Author

Pain & Peace
*Breathe_*
Change Your Mind & Heal: A Spiritual and Psychological
Guide
With Thanks

Contents

A Spark

A spark amongst the tinder,

Ignited –

Though I linger,

In the feeling of

trepidation no longer.

Surrounded by the warmth, that propels me further,

Into the existence I will.

And with that will comes hope and creation –

Quite simply, a blending of cause, correlation;

Igniting my soul afire through a spark –

Provided by those,

Who helped light my path.

Strength

I have never known a stronger person,

A heart so kind, a soul so immersed with love.

Your talents are quite often unspoken,

But given light,

Match the brightness and warmth of the sun.

'Mum' may be a simple word,

Its meanings taken for granted,

But always know, your efforts

And unconquerable spirit

Are privately lauded.

Thank you for the gifts you've given,

Thank you for the lessons;
And thank you for being able,
To teach, and learn, and listen.

For Mum, 23/11/22.

Greying

'To silver!' some may say,

As they cheer gained life wisdom,

Witnessed amongst the once-chestnut hair,

That sits upon a crown.

Others recoil, concerned to fade out,

Wishing to fall like a star –

They do not know better.

Each day is a gift,

And who can shout at the sun?

As it sets into hues of gold.

But long may that glow linger,

To better reflect

The worthiness of growing old.

And let's not forget,

Beneath a wizened crown,

A youthful mind and heart lay within –

Knowledge reserved for those who arrive,

Armed with stories and scars and a grin.

For Dad, on his birthday, 21/11/22.

Embrace

Your warmth envelops

All that is me.

My broken past,

My journey up,

And who I have become.

I didn't expect

Transcendental love,

Because of my vulnerability

And effort.

I thank you for

This sweet embrace,

That places me

In safety.

Like a soul protected
In its mother's womb –
No danger present,
And complete acceptance.

I lull amidst the pride I feel,
Gifted by your genuine zeal,
Reminding me of love's true state –
A freeing hold,
A true embrace.

With Thanks

I sit – and dream

Of brighter things;

Allowing it to fill me.

Consumed by gratitude

Of what life will be.

What is written here, will come –

By hands ethereal,

It is done.

Through the Night

I'm making my wins with gratitude and grace,
With surrender of how, and all trust in faith.
I've discovered through hard work, this is the only way,
To make it through the night.

Every time I feel lost, I'm just making my way,
To a new path, a new truth, a new dawning of day,
And even when scared, I know it's the way,
To make it through the night.

We have to fall down sometimes, let it out,
Then gather to stand, and walk through the doubt,
Release the fears, the pain, let it fade –

There's no love without grief, they're both one and the same.

So remember, when hurt, tired, and worn,
The world will keep turning, and changes will come,
No hope is ever! lost when it's held –
You will make it through the long night.

Full Circle

I wish that I could reach through time
And put my arms around you,
On nights you died a thousand times,
'Til sleep finally took you.

I wish that I could reach through space,
My hands upon your shoulders,
As you stood searching your own face,
For comfort, seeking solace.

I know that I can't turn back time,
I know I cannot reach you,
But thank you for not giving up;
Your strength has seen us both through.

Create

Sit with me, in this space

And time we share together.

Whilst leafing through the pages

On a dimmed screen.

The magic we create when we put a pen to paper,

Or any way we make our thoughts immortal,

Creates a monologue of words,

Emotions, curiously tethered.

But reading this creates a bond,

Unique in its experience,

As understanding as you will,

Will differ amongst all.

So, sit with me within this space,
And share some time together.
Create a moment that will last,
Thus, honouring a shared pleasure.

A Risk

A calculated jump,

Not blindly, into bliss.

A risk we all must take –

Without it,

There's no hope

For a better tomorrow.

Believing in ourselves,

And trusting in each other,

Are the keys to a kingdom

That holds the freedom,

And triumph,

We call love.

Holding Space

We're all a single being,
Spread out through time and space,
A thread runs through our chakras,
Connecting every face,

That often hides our feelings,
Yet all of us are free,
If we choose to become what
We're exactly meant to be.

I ask you please do listen,
Take heed and gently trace,
Your path from whence you came from,

That single, common place,

That binds us by creation,
And frees our choice with grace,
To cradle hearts of brother, sister –
For them, we're holding space.

Dreams

I keep my dreams in a jar by the bed.

When I lay my head down, I breathe...

Gratitude for the day that's passed,

Gratitude for the moment,

And thankfulness for the good to come;

May it last, my blessings abundant.

Flow

Flow, like water.

Change, overcome.

Formless, adapt to any obstacle,

Be the river –

Transcend, become.

Dewdrop

The motion unbending,

Forever unending,

Like a dewdrop,

Pooling on a lake,

That becomes one with us;

Then a cloud, then the rain,

Until, it is a dewdrop again.

Manifest

I sit, a flame, a brightening spark,

Manifesting my destiny,

Offering –

A key to my heart.

But what will thou do with freedom's gift?

Perchance, you'll be kind?

An everlasting kiss?

I manifest the chance,

Of all of this.

Then and Now

Windswept, I walk.
Embraced by memories –
Fields of gold that carry me
to the sunlight in your eyes.

A crown of daisies sits aloft your hair,
And my breath is taken, willingly.
For immeasurable moments, I exist back there;
And here, simultaneously.

It's this, remembering love's first kiss –
that gifts a stolen breath returned,
And fills my lungs with hope,
For all the time remaining.

Mask

If we are each of us, but actors,

And the whole world's but a stage,

Then who is the director?

And who put pen to page?

If you keep a mask beside your bed,

To don every day,

Before you leave your authentic self,

In stead, along your way –

How can someone befriend you?

And do you know your truth?

What happens when the mask you wear

Grows real and becomes you?

If you are but an actor,
Your life, a story told,
At least remain authentic
To the play, as it unfolds.

I Am Not Alone

I am not alone my friend,

I have you hearing me, through time,

Regardless of what has passed –

I am here with you.

So, you are not alone too.

I am not alone –

I have the wind, the stars, and the beating of my heart to keep me company.

All remind me,

I am part of one living organism.

I am not alone my friend,

For I have reached through this page

And pulled you to me.

As I write,

So do you read.

Therefore,

We are not alone.

One Day

One day, someone you love

Will hold you, tenderly,

And, embracing you,

Whisper that everything will be alright,

As they trace their palm across your shoulders,

In an unmistakable show of appreciation.

And you will cry, as you thought you'd never feel this again;

Your once broken heart,

Gently held, 'til it mends.

When I Pray

When I pray for sleep,

Do you think the birds hear me?

As they welcome the new rising sun.

When I pray for peace,

Does the wind carry my dreams?

As it stirs up and rustles the fallen, coloured leaves.

When I pray for love,

Does my heart beat to the sun?

As it both gives and takes from our lives.

When I pray for health,

Is it selfish to prioritise self?

As more are suffering greater.

Or,

When I pray at all,
Does the essence of my call,
Serve to repair the strands
That once lay severed?

As if you pray for you,
Or your health, or for love too,
It only adds to the force we know,
As common good.

Sway

Sway, bend,

Move with the breeze,

Whether it's forceful

Or gentle,

Be like the tree.

Recognise your roots are strong,

And they may remain steadfast.

The rest of you, though,

Must belong,

To the things you cannot change.

So, in order to survive, sustain,

Ensure you bend, so you won't break.

You may be strained for a short time,

But life is long, and life you have,

From swaying with the gusts.

What Comes to Pass

We cannot know what tomorrow may bring,
Nor even the following moments –
Can't change by watching the pendulum swing,
Even if it does with importance.

No garnering truth of what comes to pass,
And less than no use for the worry –
It's better to live knowing you tried your best,
And did so without feeling cornered.

The future's not known by tick-ticking time,
As it flows through hourglass' with abandon –
The concept was not of itself, it's man-made,

To describe, organise, and determine.

The knowledge we seek, of what comes to pass,
Despite the fact we can't know –
The grandfather clock, with pendulum, rocks,
And what comes to pass, will then show.

Invictus

If one could reach a million miles,
Across the depth of space and time,
A mother's arms would span beyond,
To hold you when you don't feel strong,
Support you when it all feels wrong,
And applaud you for having heart,
And being your genuine self.

Cause neither time, nor veil, nor space,
That seem to separate us,
Could every truly pull away
Our Mother's love – Invictus.

Reclaiming Peace

Staring at vacated cobwebs,

That cling, with a wisp, to the ceiling.

Waiting for sleep to come;

Not yet arrived

Is that peaceful, serene, and calm feeling.

Worry for nothings, that bounce in my mind,

Like crazed, enthused dancers of chaos,

Twisting, and yelling their uncertain rhymes,

Behind veils, in tongues sibylline.

Nothing will stop the time as it steps,

Forward, with petulant motion –

But perhaps those audible vicious torments,

Will get lost like a drop amongst oceans.

And so, I declare, to things I can't change,
And further, to misfiring circuits –
Enough, I don't care to suffer your hells,
It's time I exist in the present.

I exhale and see all my worries released,
Anxiety cannot reside here.
The thoughts I select, now reclaim my peace –
It's done; I am free, full of cheer.

Wordless

A shape, and feeling,
Defined by the melting
Of the colours of nothing,
Yet containing all rainbows.

Emotion, form, thoughtless,
Yet thoughtful;
A breaking of a wave
On a star-formed stone.

Dispersing, soundless,
A million galaxies away,
Creating, when seen, a feeling,
That can't quite be named.

. . .

Yet named it shall be,

As intelligence demands,

Reaching through time,

To come up –

Wordless.

New World

Inhale love,

Exhale rust.

Inhale hope,

Exhale mistrust.

Let go of all that does not serve

The oneness that is us,

Let go of all that does not serve

The hope in which we trust.

Inhale love,

Exhale rust.

Inhale faith,

Expel the dust.

．．．

A new world is a buildin',
Beneath the ground; its roots are strong.
They're growing over steel and concrete,
And all that was made wrong.

A new world is now dawning,
Open your eyes and see,
A new way to live, upon our mother,
Our father, blessed be.

So work with me and meditate,
Gravitate, levitate.
Boots on ground that serve no purpose
Aren't a common soul.

A new world is upon us
And it renews all that was old –

Inhale love,
Exhale rust.
Inhale hope,
Expel the dust.

Weight

All of us; we wake to greet the day

At different times, from different places.

We take a face from our dreams –

Our vision of self,

And don it, to show to everyone else

What our life is.

I think no one, or very few,

Would choose a life not happy.

You and I, burden free,

And smiling –

What a dream it is!

We try! We do. But human life

Adds little pieces of weight
To our minds.
Not enough to fracture –
But perhaps fray, if you're unlucky.

Things may add up, and take their toll,
As the warrior with a wounded soul
Shows lines and strain –
Highly strung,
Like towels grow rough when over-rung –
Over time.

The world adds weight in many ways,
And all of us want better days,
So who will stand to share the load?
To wear that burden, ease that toll?

And can you when you are the same?
Or can we only give it to the name
Of what we call existence?

We Will Not Break

We will not break, my friend –

The human spirit,

Has no end

Of strength to draw upon.

When things get rough,

The soul gets tough,

Emboldened by its knowledge –

That it's supported endlessly

By all who came before it.

So, when you're down,

Please take heart –

Your ancestors are with you.

Reminding you you're not alone,

With strength that's channelled for you.

Trying

A tentative success –

Or at least,

You tried your best.

And that is all that counts

When you're measured by a test –

That you've truly given everything,

When trying.

About the Author

Dan Sage is a creative of many colours. As a musician, poet, writer, radio announcer, and social justice advocate he takes audiences of one or many on sojourns of spiritual philosophy. Through difficult truths and occasional hard-earned cynicism shine his unquenchable spark of hope, solace and simple gratitude.

– N. Jones

If you enjoyed this book, please consider leaving a review with your retailer so that others may also enjoy it. Thank you!

Also by Dan Sage

Pain & Peace: A brief introductory poetry collection that exhibits the duality of being, introducing the reader to Dan's suite on healing.

Breathe_: A substantive collection of nearly 70 poems that witnesses the transformative healing journey, from dark to light.

Change Your Mind & Heal: A Spiritual and Psychological Guide: An activity-oriented self-help guide on how to heal through trauma, honour yourself, and improve your life, using spiritual and psychological philosophies and practices.